The Power of
PRAYER
MEETINGS

PETER MASTERS

SWORD & TROWEL
METROPOLITAN TABERNACLE
LONDON

THE POWER OF PRAYER MEETINGS

© Peter Masters 1995

SWORD & TROWEL
Metropolitan Tabernacle
Elephant & Castle
London SE1 6SD
ISBN 1 899046 10 0

Cover design by Andrew Sides

All rights reserved. No part of this publication may be reproduced or transmitted in any form or by any means, electronic or mechanical, including photocopy, recording, or any information storage and retrieval system, without permission in writing from the publisher.

Printed in Great Britain

The Power of Prayer Meetings

Two kinds of meeting

IN ORDER TO GRASP the unique place of a church prayer meeting we must appreciate that there were two distinct types of service in the early church, a pattern still followed today. There were the more public gatherings for worship and instruction which are referred to at length in *1 Corinthians 14*. These meetings were 'led' by people who were members of the pastoral or teaching team in the church, which in those days included prophets and 'junior' prophets (the tongues-speakers), who functioned alongside the pastors and teachers. These constituted a platform party, and led the worship in accordance with Paul's rules for an ordered, pre-arranged, premeditated and harmonious service (according to the strong terms used in *1 Corinthians 14.33* and *40*). They were undoubtedly all men, for Paul insists on this *(1 Corinthians 14.34-35)*.

However, there was also another, rather different, kind of meeting convened by the New Testament churches, this being the prayer meeting. It was less 'public' and probably less formal. It apparently contained no teaching element, and all those attending were believers. It was often convened in a hurry, by way of response to some pressing crisis, and there is every indication that both men and women participated. We must briefly trace the history of this meeting held specifically for prayer and see how different it was in character from the worship-teaching services.

Such a meeting first appears in the pages of *Acts* shortly before Pentecost. It was the gathering of disciples held in an upper room in Jerusalem. 'These all continued with one accord in prayer and supplication, with the women, and Mary the mother of Jesus, and with his brethren' *(Acts 1.14)*. The text does not explicitly say that the women prayed aloud, but it is expressed in a rather unguarded way if they did not.

The next recorded prayer meeting is in *Acts 4.24*, when Peter and John reported to the disciples how the chief priests had commanded them not to speak in the name of Christ. Although this may have been a gathering of apostles only, it does not lose its value as a precedent because the activities of apostles (aside from their revelatory and sign-ministry activities) constitute an example to be followed. Faced with a serious threat to the testimony, they joined together in prayer.

The same thing happened when Herod arrested Peter *(Acts 12.5)*, and prayer was made without ceasing by the church for him. We read particularly of the meeting held at the house of Mary the mother of John, where many were gathered together praying.

The principle of shared prayer between ordinary believers is supremely established by the Lord Jesus in the very well-known words of *Matthew 18.19-20* – 'Again I say unto you, That if two of you shall agree on earth as touching any thing that they shall ask, it shall be done for them of my Father which is in heaven.' These passages, and others, form the basis of this booklet, focusing on the special privileges and rules of church prayer meetings.

The special status of prayer meetings

C. H. Spurgeon certainly captured the common attitude in churches when he chose the title of his famous exhortation to prayer – *Only a Prayer Meeting!* Why, he implied, did many believers fail to grasp the momentous significance of the prayer meeting?

To this day the prayer meeting is the least regarded gathering in the church programme. Pastors frequently complain that numerous members *never* attend, while others are more often absent than present. It is undoubtedly the least significant and the least popular meeting in numerous churches. At a theoretical level, most believers agree that the prayer meeting is the 'power-house' of the church. But how many *really* think this is so? If they did, all church prayer meetings would be packed.

These pages are intended to inspire a greater sense of the importance of prayer meetings. Why does the Lord want us to pray together? Is this a biblical duty, or is it optional? What difference does it make whether we pray privately, or as a company? Will an undersized meeting really blight the work of an otherwise earnest church? What form should the prayer meeting ideally take? And what should be the style and content of prayer? In answering these questions, our starting point will be two Old Testament texts. Then we shall examine the Saviour's command for corporate prayer.

In *Isaiah 56.7* there is a prophetic text on this subject. God states that the future Gospel-age Church will be characterised by communal prayer. He says: 'For mine house shall be called an house of prayer for all people.' This is clearly about when the gentiles shall hear the Word and be converted. They, says the Lord, shall rejoice 'in my house of prayer'. It is the will of our Lord and Redeemer that His people should be conspicuous for their praying together. This is why the churches of former Soviet lands call their chapels 'Prayer Houses'. In this *Isaiah* passage the Lord presents the ministry of corporate prayer as an outstanding sign that people have been truly converted. What will be the best evidence of conversion in Gospel days? The churches will be known for prayer. Believers will flock to pray, says the Lord, and it will give them great pleasure and assurance.

In *Ezekiel 36.37* we read, 'Thus saith the Lord God; I will yet for this be enquired of by the house of Israel, to do it for them; I will increase them with men like a flock.' This text also is a prophecy about how God will work in the age of the Christian Church – the Gospel age. He will bless His people with many converts – provided they pray. Without the prayers of the house of Israel (symbolising the people of God acting together) He will not bless them. 'Ye have not,' says James, 'because ye ask not.' The Lord longs to honour our evangelistic efforts. But there may be an obstacle, causing Him to hold back His blessing. Have we pleaded with Him in prayer?

Of course, it is the business of the individual Christian to pray for the blessing of God upon the work of the Gospel. But this text shows that God's people must also pray as a 'house'. Supremely, it is the business of a church fellowship, the people gathered together. They must pray as a body or a unit. The *Ezekiel* text shows that the prayer of the *group* is particularly instrumental. It has an effect. *Israel* must pray for *Israel's* blessing. Today the *congregation* must pray for blessing upon the *congregation*.

Do we really appreciate the spiritual uniqueness of meetings for prayer? Perhaps we think this is just a matter of arithmetic. If one person can be effective in prayer, then a number of people will do even better. Is this our understanding of how it works? Is a prayer meeting merely a multiplicity of people joining forces to increase prayer strength? Is it simply a matter of applying the old rule – what one can do, two can do better? If this is our view, then we have missed the point, for there is much more to it than that.

Here is one of *the* fundamental principles of Scripture, and one so crucial, that all believers should grasp it and glory in it. The principle is that Almighty God, for special reasons, has ordained as a duty the practice of communal, corporate prayer for His people, and has attached unique promises to this duty. Is my church a house of prayer? Does it fulfil the Lord's desire? Do I grasp that I have been cemented by the bonds of a covenant into a *praying* family?

Look, for a moment, at the literal sense behind those beautiful words – 'I will yet . . . be enquired of . . . ' The Hebrew means, 'I will yet be *tracked*, pursued, searched after.' The kind of prayer referred to here is not easy. Great effort and earnestness is suggested. The Lord must be asked with persistence. He must almost be pursued and persuaded. The Lord requires His people to desire very greatly the things for which they pray, and to plead for them.

A little knowledge is a dangerous thing, and sometimes when believers first come to see more of God's sovereignty, they lose some of their fervour in prayer. Having discovered that all things are foreordained, they think that they should now pray only one prayer – that God's will should be done. They no longer feel that their prayers will make any difference. Surely, they say, if God has ordained that a sick believer will die, he will die. If God has decided to save, He will save. How can we change predestined events? The truth is that God urges and commands us to pray and assures us that our prayers *will* make a difference. But how? The explanation is that God has foreordained our prayer, as well as His response. The God Who calls and moves us to pray, will not ignore our prayers. Our praying is all part of His glorious, predestinating plan.

Or we may look at it another way. When God, in eternity past, predetermined all things, He took account of the future prayers of His people. He listened in His Eternal Council! God's children have an amazing privilege. They have access to the *eternal* throne. They may prevail upon their heavenly Father! His ear is and has been open to their cry from eternity. Prayer is truly instrumental, and especially corporate prayer.

Every great blessing in the life of a church and in the life of an individual is obtained through prayer. Even salvation, initiated and accomplished by a sovereign work of the Spirit, is not consciously tasted without prayer. The Spirit regenerates us, inclines our will, and brings us to the place of repentance. It is all a work of grace! If God did not perform that work within us, we would never desire or seek Him. And yet, in the mystery of His will, He works in such a way that we voluntarily, freely, longingly cry out for pardon and new life. But for God's regenerating work, we would never ask. And without asking, salvation would never be ours.

We learn from our conversion, therefore, that every great blessing must be asked for. This principle is illustrated throughout the Bible. This is why the Bible is such a large book. It is the record of people in deep need crying out to the Lord for deliverance and receiving His blessing.

The children of Israel sighed by reason of their bondage, and their cry came up unto God. He caused them, stubborn and stiff-necked people as they were, to cry out, and plead for help. Only then did He bless them. Moses prayed, and cried earnestly, and what was the result? The waters of the Red Sea parted before the people. Elijah cried out for the rain, and it came. Throughout church history, the story is the same. All the great awakenings and reformations have begun with the Lord waking up souls to pray for these things.

We may make many mistakes in the Christian life, but the worst is to leave out prayer, because then we cannot receive any great blessings. Without prayer, we lack any deep experience of God, and any significant interventions in our lives. What is true of individuals, is true also of churches: no prayer, no blessing!

Christ's command and promise

The most direct passage of all on the subject of corporate prayer is the great promise of Christ recorded in *Matthew 18.19-20*. Though expressed as a promise, it is really a command and a direction. Indeed, it is nothing less than an ordinance. The Lord said: 'I say unto you, That if two of you shall agree on earth as touching any thing that they shall ask, it shall be done for them of my Father which is in heaven. For where two or three are gathered together in my name, there am I in the midst of them.' When the Lord uttered these words, He was instructing the disciples about church affairs, particularly the procedure for dealing with misconduct in the church. He was not speaking to a casual handful of believers, as though giving an optional prayer opportunity to those who wished to meet informally (although His promise certainly includes this). He was giving official instructions to His churches. He was inaugurating the duty of corporate prayer. It is clear that He is not speaking about a worship service, with preaching, but about a prayer meeting. He said that whatever the church would pray for in a united way, however few the members, their prayers would be heard by the Father, and Christ would be in their midst.

This promise had an immediate application to the matter in hand – discipline. Whenever a congregation needed guidance to deal with a lapse of godliness, then God would help them, and their elders, if they prayed. However, the words of Christ are by no means limited to the subject of offences and discipline. They apply to 'any thing that they shall ask'. The promise covers *all* the needs of the church.

We are now looking at the teaching of Christ that there is *special power* in the prayer of God's people when they are assembled together. The promise is made to the smallest plural company possible – two people. We believe in the infallible utterances of the Lord. We want to understand them accurately, and to act on them fully. What *exactly* are we commanded to do by the Lord? We are promised a special hearing when we *agree* about anything we shall ask. What does the word *agree* mean here? In the Greek, it is a word of enormous significance.

The Greek word *(sumphoneo)* literally means – to sound together. That is the briefest way of translating it. The Lord said, 'If any two of you shall sound together . . . ' 'Agree' is a correct translation, but the word goes deeper than that. It is a word used to describe instruments playing harmoniously together. It is also used in the New Testament to describe the way in which two people verbally strike a bargain. In the vineyard parable of *Matthew 20,* for instance, the keeper of the vineyard *agrees* with the labourers, and this is the word used. They bartered, and then came to an agreement audibly.

When used about prayer, this word refers to *prayers spoken aloud.* It is audible prayer, not silent prayer. It is not a matter of different people praying aloud at the same time, because there can be no intelligent agreement in that. In this 'sounding together', one prays, and the others follow silently, winging those desires heavenward along with the one who prays aloud. The Lord's people subordinate themselves one to another, and lead one another in prayer. Upon *such* prayer there is the unique favour of God.

Agreement obviously implies more than the act of following one another's audible prayers. The instruments of an orchestra cannot play together without prior agreement about what they will play. Equally, agreement in prayer extends backwards to before the praying begins. A church prayer meeting is not a time for surprises, shocks, novelties and innovations. It is not an opportunity for individuals to bang particular drums, or promote causes that may not be in accord with the concerns of the whole prayer meeting. It is certainly not a time for the airing of complaints. This is a gathering in which we will be agreed. We will have an 'agenda', and common desires, and pray in agreement for those things. Agreement will be the controlling principle of the occasion.

Sometimes when believers gather for prayer, some enterprising person thinks it is an ideal opportunity to introduce to the church some unheard-of idea of his own, or even to reprove (in prayer, of course!) the people of God, or to protest about something. Clearly, all this is out of order, because the aim is to be at one in the things for which we are praying. If someone feels there is a problem in the church, or is burdened about some new thing that could be done, the matter should be taken up with the officers in the proper way, and not catapulted directly into the prayer meeting.

To return to the Lord's inauguration of prayer meetings – are we among the many true Christians who opt out of the church prayer meeting, and throw away the Lord's promises? Do we deprive our church of its full share of instrumentality and blessing by our failure to support the prayer meeting? Perhaps, as sincere, born-again people, we just need a little more convincing that it really is the will of God. Can we be certain that the Lord meant *all* His people to gather for prayer? Of course we can, because there are no elite groups in the Christian church. If the Lord calls for corporate prayer from His people, we may be certain that *all* will be called to it, not just some. It could not be that a privileged few would be given superior promises for prayer. The doctrine of the priesthood of all believers teaches that the duty of prayer is the same for all.

Beyond all doubt the Saviour intended that all should join in the form of prayer to which He attached special promises. We must never interpret away our obligation to the prayer gathering, and make it an optional exercise. Powerful confirmation of the fact that corporate prayer is the duty of all is found in the practice of the early church. *They* realised that meetings for communal prayer were for all.

When the disciples gathered in an upper room in Jerusalem for the first recorded prayer meeting of the young church, there was no doubt in their minds that prayer gatherings were for all. We read – 'These all continued with one accord in prayer and supplication, with the women, and Mary the mother of Jesus, and with his brethren' *(Acts 1.14)*. This had not been the Jewish way of going on. It was not merely a continuation of custom or culture. Even before the fulness of revelation was available about conduct in the church, they realised that corporate prayer is for all.

Fourteen years later, another prayer meeting is recorded, undoubtedly typical of their regular gatherings. *Acts 12.5* tells us: 'Peter therefore was kept in prison: but prayer was made without ceasing of the church unto God for him.' When Peter was released by the angel of the Lord, 'he came to the house of Mary the mother of John, whose surname was Mark; where many were gathered together praying' (verse 12). C. H. Spurgeon, commenting on this event, says that Peter thought to himself, 'Where shall I go?' Then he remembered that it was prayer meeting night down at John Mark's mother's house. That was the place to go. They were not gathered to hear a sermon, but to pray. This was the business on hand. And 'many' were gathered – a great rebuke to numerous believers today. By practice, by conviction and by instinct the people of God gathered together to pray for great matters. Here was a crowded meeting, continuing well after midnight, with both men and women. The early church certainly knew that the Saviour had ordained corporate prayer for all.

Many churches today combine their weekly prayer meeting with their Bible study, which is obviously better than having no prayer meeting at all. However, C. H. Spurgeon was strongly critical of this arrangement, which was a new habit in Victorian times. He could not understand why churches should want to do this, and asked how a combined meeting could do justice to either purpose. The ideal is to have separate meetings on different evenings, and it is certainly the case that where churches implement this, they reap a blessing. (A major *incidental* blessing is also theirs, because with two weeknight meetings parents of young families are able to attend on an alternating basis, so that each is able to be present at one of the two meetings every week.)

The purposes of the Lord in requiring corporate prayer

If believers could only see the mighty purposes served, they would surely discard with shame all their complacency and indifference toward the prayer meeting. If they could only grasp that it is the product of divine wisdom, they would surely pledge themselves to its support. Why has the Lord ordained corporate prayer? Why is corporate prayer uniquely necessary?

1. To demonstrate dependence on God's power

First, the prayer meeting is ordained by God to provide a clear and emphatic demonstration of our complete dependence upon His power for all our work. Of course, we call upon the Lord in worship services, though not for quite the same things, nor in such detail, nor by means of many voices. To convene separately for the sole purpose of bringing the work of the church before the Lord signals our dependence upon Him as nothing else could do. At the same time, the prayer meeting sets before members a demonstration of the answering power of God.

Supposing a church held no prayer gathering, and individuals undertook the entire ministry of prayer in the privacy of their homes. If God were to bless on this basis, and wonderful things were to happen, the members would not necessarily connect them with the prayers of the fellowship, for they would be unaware of them. God, therefore, has organised it differently. He has ordained that we should come together and audibly share in crying out for great needs and blessings. Then, when the divine response is revealed, it is obvious to all that God is at work, and He has answered prayer. We shall all say that we cried out to Him, and He heard us from on high, and we shall give Him the glory.

We see this key aspect of the prayer meeting – that it is a

demonstration of dependence upon God – in that grand term 'house of prayer'. Corporate prayer makes praying a central and recognisable feature of the Christian community. It is therefore a vital part of the ministry of a church to mount this act of dependence upon God, partly for the benefit of its members, and also as a testimony to all who come into its circle of influence. Every person who has some link, however tenuous, with a live church will perceive that it meets for prayer, and consequently experiences the response of the Lord. God desires that every church should have a prayer meeting as a prominent witness, so that His glory should be promoted in all hearts.

2. *To focus minds on the church*

Secondly, the prayer gathering is required by the Lord and necessary because it trains the people of God to be concerned about the fellowship and ministries of their local church. God, after all, is not just dealing with us as individuals. He delights to mould entire church fellowships. He desires to shape and beautify the whole membership together, and to bring about a responsible and involved body of people. There is nothing quite like the prayer meeting for promoting and advancing this. We *care* together in the prayer meetings, and we *feel* together. We take responsibility for the work both at home and overseas. We focus our minds on the needs and burdens, and we spread them before the Lord. We are all vitally concerned, and share the prayers of one another.

We note the strong emphasis on the local church as a *body* in the New Testament. The apostle Paul tells us that so much growth and sanctification is effected through 'the whole body fitly joined together' *(Ephesians 4.16).* Communal or corporate prayer is an essential part of this ministry of the whole body.

In the prayer gathering, preoccupation with ourselves as individual believers slips away, and we become a group of people longing for the blessing of others, and for the prosperity of the cause. We learn also to have concern for the trials of other servants of the Lord, and to rejoice at their triumphs as God answers prayer. How typical of God's handiwork, that He should devise a way of combining prayer with our sanctification! In the prayer gathering we are refined and honed as a united body of people.

Such a work inevitably draws us together. Those who fight together against a powerful enemy are always drawn together, and the prayer gathering (as far as sincere people are concerned) draws believers together almost as nothing else can. It cements unions, and promotes respect. We hear each other pray; we subordinate ourselves to each other; we appreciate each other. We feel, as the old saying goes, one another's spirits, and we are warmed and deepened in oneness and regard. To adopt a well-worn phrase, the church that prays together, stays together. The church where large numbers pray together will never be an unfeeling group of uncommitted, half-Christians! Where the prayer meeting flourishes, there will be no lack of sensitive hearts and willing volunteers for the work of the Lord. The church prayer meeting exerts a profound influence for good!

3. To extend faith's horizons

Thirdly, the prayer meeting is ordained by God and necessary because it trains the church to develop faith, confidence and anticipation for *great* things. The Lord said to the disciples while at the well of Sychar, 'Lift up your eyes, and look on the fields; for they are white already to harvest' *(John 4.35)*. The prayer meeting has the same effect as that exhortation. It makes us lift up our eyes to the harvest. Just think what united prayer achieves. It focuses the minds of the people upon larger-scale blessings, namely, God's dealings with a whole congregation. It lifts our horizons to a higher sphere, and this, incidentally, gives us a better perspective for our personal circumstances.

The church prayer meeting has a long list of high matters to bring before the Lord. It has issues of enormous significance, such as the reaching of entire towns, and the saving of all their children from the jaws of atheism. It has on its agenda matters of momentous importance to vast numbers of souls. Its scope ranges to the highest reaches of spiritual warfare.

There is nothing to equal a worthy prayer gathering for delivering believers from spiritual mediocrity. Left to ourselves and our private prayers we may possibly descend to 'small-thinking'. We may become entirely trapped within a world of personal concerns, and strictly domestic or local matters. The prayer meeting takes us out of all that, and sets us in a 'large place', from where we can see the greater harvest, and pray for the 'greater works'.

4. To provide schooling in prayer

Fourthly, the prayer meeting is required and necessary because it is by *corporate* prayer that believers discover the full scope, range and manner of prayer. United prayer is uniquely educational and broadening. In the prayer meeting individuals are taken outside their own style of prayer. Undemonstrative believers learn to appreciate passionate pleading, and so on. Friends who are given to generalising learn to value specific praying. All are carried into unexplored regions of both subject and expression, and are thereby schooled in the whole science of pleading with God. Those who could not personally pray in a particular way, do so by following the audible prayers of others. Is this part of God's purpose for the prayer meeting? Yes indeed, because Scripture says so. In *1 Corinthians 12.7* we read that 'the manifestation of the Spirit is given to every man to profit withal.' In other words, any spiritual gift given to one, is for the profit of all, and the gift of prayer is no exception. All share, all learn, all benefit.

The young in faith learn the ways of prayer, and those who are older in the faith gain a broader grasp. What a remarkable institution the prayer gathering is! What a means, also, of promoting godly humility! Here we find all kinds of people humbling themselves before the Lord as a company. The ministers, the office bearers, the intellectuals, the respected and the aged stand shoulder to shoulder, as it were, with the youngest believers to acknowledge their complete dependence upon the power of the Holy Spirit, and to labour in prayer.

Are we frustrating the Lord's purposes for His people by our absence from the prayer meeting? Are we depriving our church of our prayer-labour, depriving our fellow believers of our fellowship in prayer, and depriving ourselves of the effects which this meeting is designed to have on our own souls? Is our attendance, at best, spasmodic or inconsistent? If it is, then the Lord is offended, and the church is wounded. Can we appreciate the divine purposes behind this meeting? Has it slipped out of our minds that prayer meetings were designed, not by Christians, but by God? It is Christ Who has ordained the duty of corporate prayer. May all sincere believers yield themselves afresh to the Lord in the regular support of their church prayer meeting, so that they and their churches may reap a new scale of blessing upon their work and witness.

What should we pray for?

What kind of prayers are appropriate for the church prayer meeting? The words of Christ point us in the right direction. He said, 'If two of you shall agree on earth as touching any thing that they shall ASK . . .' The meeting ordained by Christ is first and foremost an *asking* meeting. To keep this vital point in view, past generations of Christians have actually called the prayer meeting 'the asking meeting'. The Greek word *ask* means just this. It means beg, call for, crave, desire, make supplication, and require. The prayer meeting is chiefly to focus on things that we need.

Obvious though this may seem, it often slips out of view. Instead of asking for specific needs to be met ('things' is the Lord's word), well-meaning friends sometimes concentrate on extolling His great

3.1). We are also to pray for protection for the church, for the Lord commanded the disciples, 'Watch and pray, that ye enter not into temptation: the spirit indeed is willing, but the flesh is weak' *(Matthew 26.41).*

We are to pray for labourers to bring in the lost, both in our home church and elsewhere, for the Lord said, 'The harvest truly is plenteous, but the labourers are few; pray ye therefore the Lord of the harvest, that he will send forth labourers into his harvest' *(Matthew 9.37-38).* We are to pray for the blessing of God on all the departments and all the missionaries of the church, not merely listing them, but mentioning the special efforts and difficulties of each. If we pray about obstacles and trials, the Lord will make bare His arm, and see the workers through triumphantly, in due time.

Few things are more disappointing in a prayer meeting than to hear the same catalogue-style prayers from the same people each week. If it is apparent to *us* that they have no close concern about the departments for which they pray, how much more obvious it will be to the searching eye of the Lord. Let us pray for *real* matters, and the Lord will hear us.

Of course, there are many other vital subjects for prayer. We must pray for our sick, for those who are in bonds for the sake of the Gospel, for the Sunday School, for the preachers and officers, for the country, and so many other 'things' besides.

How should we pray?
1. With great feeling and earnestness

It is important to review some aspects of *how* we should pray in a prayer meeting. First, we should pray *believingly* and *earnestly*. We should believe in the real instrumentality and effectiveness of prayer, as we considered earlier. We should pray as those who truly believe that Christ is present and the Father is listening. Without high drama, but with real desire, we must pray as children who long to prevail on their Father.

A well-known American televangelist used to feature on his programme an altar, built from thousands of envelopes containing prayer requests from viewers. The writers all suffered from some form of illness, and all sought a word of healing from the programme's host. At a given point in the service, this man would walk up to the altar of letters, wave his hand over the place, and announce in a brisk, matter-of-fact voice that he was about to pray for the sick. He would then, in a tone of indifference, and without bothering to close his eyes, mutter one sentence of prayer, and promptly stride away, claiming that all would be healed. There was no labouring in prayer, nor any detectable concern for the afflicted, or their recovery.

How different from the Lord, Who taught the disciples at the healing of a demonised child, 'This kind goeth not out but by prayer and fasting' *(Matthew 17.21)*. In the Garden of Gethsemane, the Lord – 'being in an agony . . . prayed more earnestly' *(Luke 22.44)*. Even for the Lord, Who had unceasing and perfect fellowship with the Father, there were degrees in prayer. (This text implies at least two – earnestly, and more earnestly.)

Should we pray easy, relaxed, effortless, matter-of-fact prayers? Should we pray in the tone of voice more suited to leaving a message on an answerphone? Earnestness and feeling is the hallmark of real prayer, and the greater the need, the greater should be that earnestness. That is the example of the One Who taught His disciples to pray.

2. *Using direct and plain language*

Secondly, prayer should always be plain. The prayers recorded in the New Testament are certainly fervent, but they are also *straightforward*. They are no match for the grand, florid productions sometimes heard today from the lips of believers! These are masterly compositions in their way, but should we pray as though the prayer meeting is a theological or literary competition? To hear some prayers, it is not surprising that young Christians are intimidated into silence. The fervour of prayer is enhanced by directness and plainness.

At a practical level, these remarks on plainness assume that the person praying can be heard. This is of particular concern in larger prayer meetings. The custom of all churches years ago was for those leading in prayer to stand, both men and women. By standing, the voice is extricated from the muffling effect of seats and clothing, and from the limiting effect of a crouching position. By this means the person with a quiet voice will be heard.

3. By means of many contributors

Thirdly, as many people as possible should pray audibly in the prayer meeting. The number of those able to participate will be governed by the time available. Whether several hundred are gathered, or several dozen, time will only allow the same number to pray aloud. If the time given for prayer is, say, forty minutes, then twelve to fifteen people may be able to pray aloud. The average contribution might be around three minutes, some a little longer, some shorter.

The more 'pastoral' aspects of prayer would naturally fall to those older in the faith. In larger meetings it will not be possible for the same friends to contribute every week. However, there will probably be other opportunities, as many churches also hold pre-service prayer meetings, and still other times for corporate prayer. Those who pray at too great a length will usually respond to a private and courteous request by a pastor or leader to trim their prayers so that others may participate. Such a number of prayers naturally enables people from different departments of the work to lift their cause before the Lord. Hopefully, all stages of spiritual pilgrimage will be represented, so that in a measure, the Lord is addressed by the entire spiritual family.

To facilitate much prayer, there must be no gaps. Friends must come prepared to pray, and to pray early, so that prayer is continuous. An almost seamless prayer meeting surely expresses reverence for the Lord, and a true belief in the infinite value of such an audience. Would we lapse into time-wasting silence if we had an audience with some important and influential person on Earth?

4. Addressing prayer to the Father

Fourthly, corporate prayer should always be addressed to the Father, and offered in the name of the Lord Jesus Christ, our Saviour, for this is the example and rule of Scripture for such prayer. In *Matthew 6*, the Saviour says several times that we should address our prayers to the Father, and the pattern prayer begins, 'Our Father'. In the prayer meeting of *Acts 4.24-30*, they prayed to the Father in the name of the Son. In *Ephesians 5.20*, the rule is given – 'Giving thanks always for all things unto God and the Father in the name of our Lord Jesus Christ.' (This instruction is repeated in *Colossians 3.17*.) In *1 Peter 2.5*, the rule is given once again. Here the church fellowship, pictured as a spiritual temple, is 'to offer up spiritual sacrifices, acceptable to God *[the Father]* by Jesus Christ.' Whatever member of the Godhead believers may address in their private praying, when gathered together we should keep the 'rule of assembly', and pray to our heavenly Father.

Surely it is the *right* of our Saviour for prayer to be offered in His name! He has purchased our salvation and secured our access to the Father. We have no other plea than His shed blood and glorious righteousness. He has done everything for us, and by Him alone we pray. Is He not entitled to be credited? It is a great shame that in these days of informality, believers sometimes fail to give glory to His name, either omitting the correct conclusion to prayer, or substituting some corner-cutting formula. Why should we want to leave out the name or titles of our Saviour?

It is not really good enough to end a prayer saying, 'We pray in Thy Son's name.' An abrupt, 'Amen,' is even worse. A novel alternative such as, 'We pray for the glory of Jesus Christ,' is better, but it misses the real point, for our prayer is only acceptable because of the name of Jesus Christ. What we should be acknowledging is that He is the sole means of our being able to pray. We must honour and adore Him for that. The very best way to conclude a prayer is with the words, 'In the name of the LORD JESUS CHRIST, our Saviour.' A shorter form is acceptable, as long as our glorious Lord is clearly acknowledged.

Does this mean that prayer-endings will sound rather samish? It does, but this means that a dozen or more times in our prayer gathering we shall acknowledge Him together. What could possibly be wrong with that? It is a glorious statement, worthy to be repeated many times. We must name His name or His titles or both (with or without sincerely meant superlatives), every time we pray, and so give Him the glory.

5. All joining in the loud 'Amen'

Fifthly, all the people should swell the loud 'Amen!' at the close of every prayer, for this is also the rule of Scripture and the example of Heaven. 'Amen' comes from the Hebrew verb to be firm or to be sure. It means 'truly' and 'let it be so'. When the Lord taught His disciples to pray, He concluded that pattern prayer with the 'Amen' *(Matthew 6.13)*. *1 Corinthians 14.16* shows that New Testament worshippers – even the uninstructed newcomers – quickly learned to say 'Amen' to the prayers publicly offered. This was nothing new. In the Old Testament, the people said, 'Amen' to make a sentiment, an oath, a promise or a prayer their own.

In *1 Chronicles 16.36,* all the people said, 'Amen' at the end of David's psalm and its concluding prayer. They did not *think* the word, but *said* it out loud. *Nehemiah 5.13* and *8.6* also show that the people were accustomed to amens, as an audible, emphatic, earnest response to vows and prayers.

In the New Testament, the amen continued to be a response of approval and agreement, following benedictions, doxologies and prayers. The Lord Himself used the word *before* making great statements of Truth, but when used by the people it was an assent of faith and commitment. Audible prayer must be endorsed with an audible response, otherwise there is no 'sounding together' as the Lord requires. A loud amen signifies attentive minds and fervent hearts. It is what the Lord desires, and it strangely knits together the people in their bond of fervent prayer.

✷ ✷ ✷

'Pray without ceasing,' says Paul. 'In every thing give thanks.' 'Faithful is he that calleth you, who also will do it.' May we prove the promises of Christ in our church prayer gatherings. May they become, in every city, town and village, occasions of power and blessing, where the first stirrings of awakening shall be felt. May the people of God everywhere be faithful, and pray without fainting, for the Lord has commanded them, and encouraged them with great promises, and what He promises, He will certainly perform.

APPENDIX:
Should Women Also Pray?

Should both men and women pray in prayer meetings? Or are women to remain silent? After all, the apostle's rule is, 'Let your women keep silence in the churches: for it is not permitted unto them to speak . . . for it is a shame for women to speak in the church' *(1 Corinthians 14.34-35)*. This rule, however, is about *teaching* (including the public questioning of teachers), for this is the subject of the passage. In *1 Timothy 2.11-12* Paul says, 'let the woman learn in silence with all subjection. But I suffer not a woman to teach, nor to usurp authority over the man, but to be in silence.' Women are to be in silence in the context of *teaching*. They should not teach, nor participate in the government of the local church. (Teaching is an expression of authority, for it is ruling by the Word.)

Neither of these scriptures prohibits women from praying aloud in prayer meetings, according to the overwhelming majority of Bible believers who take seriously the rule that they must not teach. As long as prayer does not become a cloak or disguise for preaching, women may pray alongside men.

But what about Paul's words in *1 Timothy 2.8*? Many believe that these make praying aloud in the prayer meetings an all-male prerogative. Paul says: 'I will therefore that men pray every where, lifting up holy hands, without wrath and doubting.' The Greek word used for *men* certainly refers to the male in contrast to the female. We feel certain, however, that this verse does not ban women from praying aloud, for the following reasons:

Prior to this verse, Paul has been commanding that prayer and intercession be made for all men (the Greek term here includes men and women). He has particularly urged prayer for rulers, and that people may come to the saving light of Christ, the only Mediator. In the light of this, we must look for the natural sense of his words, 'I will therefore that men pray every where.' Does he really mean to say that *only* men should do this?

To establish his meaning, we should consider two alternative meanings to see which makes logical sense.

Alternative 1: 'I exhort that prayer be made for rulers and for the evangelisation of all peoples. *For this purpose, I command that only the men pray.*'

Alternative 2: 'I exhort that prayer be made for rulers and for the evangelisation of all peoples. *For this purpose, I command that men pray in every community, without dissension and doubting.*'

It should be obvious that *Alternative 1* makes no sense. How will the evangelisation of all people be advanced if only the men pray? *Alternative 2*, however, makes very good sense. The evangelisation of the world will certainly be advanced if spiritual men pray in every community in a united, believing spirit.

The intention of Paul's command is clearly that men should pray for the spread of the Gospel *wherever God has set them*, and *in a spirit of unity*. This is not about the exclusive duty of men to pray in prayer meetings. *Alternative 1* is a meaning which is read into the verse. It is not natural, and it is not logical. Why then does Paul address this specifically to men? Because some men have a tendency to male errors, such as disunity, and some women to female errors, such as excessive concern with dress. Each sex is therefore given its own exhortation. Men must pray paying special attention to *their* weakness, and women must pray paying special attention to *theirs*.

Paul proceeds at once to say that the women *must* also pray. The next verse reads: 'In like manner also, that women adorn themselves in modest apparel . . . ' The words, 'in like manner,' connect with Paul's previous words,

'I will therefore that men pray every where.' What are women to do in like manner? They are to pray for the evangelisation of all.

Some expositors say that the words, 'in like manner,' refer back to Paul's word of command only, 'I will therefore . . . ' However, this leads to the same problem that we noted earlier. The passage ceases to be logical. Would Paul really say, 'In the light of our duty to pray for the evangelisation of all, I command that men pray everywhere . . . and I likewise command that women dress modestly for the prayer meeting'? Surely not. Both men and women are exhorted to pray.

Confirmation that this interpretation is correct is to be seen in the suddenness with which Paul raises the matter of women not being permitted to teach. He says, 'Let the woman learn in silence with all subjection. But I suffer not a woman to teach.' If Paul has just said (as we believe) that both men and women are to pray, it is to be expected that he will immediately add, 'But liberty to pray must not be taken as liberty to teach.'

We may paraphrase and expand the apostle's words in the following way:

'I likewise command the women to pray everywhere, but with modest clothing and a record of kindly deeds. However, when it comes to the teaching ministry, they must learn in silence with a teachable spirit, for I do not permit women to teach.'

Obviously, women must always respect the Lord's rules about teaching. If they are inclined to lecture, teach or exhort in their prayers, then they stray into error. Both men and women should confine themselves to 'praising' and 'asking' prayers, offered sincerely and simply, but women should be especially careful in this.

These remarks apply, of course, only to the prayer meetings. They do not apply to services for worship and preaching, which, scripturally, are 'led' services, for which the male pastor-teachers and other elders have responsibility.

Companion booklets by Dr Masters:

Your Reasonable Service for the Lord

It is a sad fact that many Bible-believing Christians do not engage in any real service for the Lord. They loyally attend meetings for worship and ministry, and may give generous financial support, but they *do* very little. This booklet focuses on the strong terms of exhortation to Christian service found in the New Testament, explaining their full meaning. Here is a challenging call to all who love the Lord.

Seven Certain Signs of True Conversion

'Are there recognisable signs that true conversion has occurred? How can seekers tell if God has worked in their hearts? Or how can Christian workers discern the spiritual standing of a seeker or inquirer, or "test" the standing of an applicant for baptism and church membership?'

This booklet is a guide to the marks of true conversion for those who doubt their salvation, and for the use of spiritual counsellors.

The Goal of Brotherly Love

The great goal is *philadelphia* love, a New Testament term indicating a depth and tenacity of love equal to the love of a blood tie. What obstructs and hinders this strong mutual affection among believers? What steps must be taken to promote and preserve it? Here is a searching treatment of a topic vital to the holiness and happiness of believers.

Tithing

Subtitled *The Privilege of Christian Stewardship*, this presents biblical principles under a series of helpful headings. All the main questions about stewardship are answered, as the author draws Christians into the full blessing of belonging to the Lord.

The Purposes of the Lord's Supper

The Saviour calls His people to regularly observe His Supper. But do we have a clear awareness of all that the Lord's Supper means? Here are nine purposes behind the Lord's Supper, providing a rich basis for thought and prayer at the Table of the Lord. A further suggested plan for reflection and prayer is drawn from Paul's words in *1 Corinthians 11.23-33*. This proposes five 'directions' in which believers should look, spiritually, in order to honour the Lord's instructions.